I See Red

Trudy Micco

Bailey Books
an imprint of
Enslow Publishers, Inc.
40 Industrial Road
Box 398
Berkeley Heights, NJ 07922
USA
http://www.enslow.com

Bailey Books, an imprint of Enslow Publishers, Inc.

Library of Congress Cataloging-in-Publication Data

Micco, Trudy.
I see red / Trudy Micco.
p. cm. — (All about colors)
Summary: "Learn about the color red"— Provided by publisher.
  Includes bibliographical references and index.
ISBN 978-0-7660-3787-8
1. Red—Juvenile literature. 2. Color—Juvenile literature. I. Title.
QC495.5.M477 2011
535.6—dc22

                                        2010011874

Paperback ISBN: 978-1-59845-162-7

Printed in the United States of America

062010 Lake Book Manufacturing, Inc., Melrose Park, IL

10 9 8 7 6 5 4 3 2 1

Photo Credits: Shutterstock.com

Cover Photo: Shutterstock.com

Note to Parents and Teachers

Help pre-readers get a jumpstart on reading. These lively stories introduce simple concepts
with repetition of words and short simple sentences. Photos and illustrations fill the pages
with color and effectively enhance the text. Free Educator Guides are available for this series
at www.enslow.com. Search for the *All About Colors* series name.

Contents

Words to Know 3

Story 5

Read More. 24

Web Sites 24

Index. 24

Words to Know

red

hat

Where is my red hat?

It is not here.

Where is my red hat?

It is not here.

Where is my red hat?

It is not here.

Where is my red hat?

It is not here.

Where is my red hat?

It is on my head!

Read More

Bruce, Lisa. *Red.* Chicago, Ill.: Raintree, 2004.

Sidman, Joyce. *Red Sings From Treetops: A Year in Colors.*
    Boston: Houghton Mifflin Books for Children, 2009.

Web Sites

Chateau MeddyBemps *A Rainbow of Frogs.*
<http://www.meddybemps.com/9.500.html>

Do2Learn. *What Color?*
<http://www.do2learn.com/games/whatcolor/pages/index.html>

Index

hat, 5, 9, 13, 17, 21

head, 23

here, 7, 11, 15, 19

red, 5, 9, 13, 17, 21

see, 23

where 5, 9, 13, 21

Guided Reading Level: **B**

Guided Reading Leveling System is based on the guidelines
recommended by Fountas and Pinnell.

Word Count: 46